Girls Science Club

Cool Chemistry Activities for Girls

by Jodi Wheeler-Toppen, PhD

Consultant:
Professor Sally Chapman
Department of Chemistry
Barnard College
New York, New York

CAPSTONE PRESS
a capstone imprint

Snap Books are published by Capstone Press,
1710 Roe Crest Drive, North Mankato, Minnesota 56003.
www.capstonepub.com

Copyright © 2012 by Capstone Press, a Capstone imprint.
All rights reserved.
No part of this publication may be reproduced in whole or in part, or stored in a retrieval system, or transmitted in any form or by any means, electronic, mechanical, photocopying, recording, or otherwise, without written permission of the publisher.
For information regarding permission, write to Capstone Press,
1710 Roe Crest Drive, North Mankato, Minnesota 56003.

 Books published by Capstone Press are manufactured with paper containing at least 10 percent post-consumer waste.

Library of Congress Cataloging-in-Publication Data
Wheeler-Toppen, Jodi.
 Cool chemistry activities for girls / by Jodi Wheeler-Toppen.
  p. cm.—(Snap books. Girls science club)
  Includes bibliographical references and index.
  Summary: "Provides step-by-step instructions for activities demonstrating chemistry concepts and scientific explanations of the concepts presented"—Provided by publisher.
  ISBN 978-1-4296-7674-8 (library binding)
  ISBN 978-1-4296-8020-2 (paperback)
  1. Chemistry—Experiments—Juvenile literature. 2. Girls—Education—Juvenile literature. I. Title.
  QD43.W44 2012
  540.78—dc23   2011020700

Editor: Jennifer Besel
Designer: Heidi Thompson
Photo Stylist: Sarah Schuette
Scheduler: Marcy Morin
Production Specialist: Kathy McColley

Photo Credits: All images Capstone Studio: Karon Dubke except: Shutterstock: Jaap Hart, cover (bottom), blue67design, cover (drawn design), haveseen, cover (top)

Printed in the United States of America in North Mankato, Minnesota.
062018   000034

Table of Contents

Girls Only 4

Festive Fountain 6

Bubblicious Fun 8

Peppermint Lip Balm 10

Vanilla-Almond Shampoo 12

Stress-Relieving Putty 14

Earth-Friendly Plastic 16

Apple-Cinnamon Air Freshener 18

Rainbow Candle Holders 20

The Great Muffin Puff 22

Sweet Jewels 26

Glossary 30

Read More 31

Internet Sites 31

Index 32

Girls Only

If you think chemistry only happens in high-tech labs, think again. From your shampoo to your jewelry, chemistry shows up in some unexpected places.

To understand chemistry, you need to start small. Everything around you is made of trillions of tiny particles called **atoms**. Atoms are so small you can't even see them under a microscope. An ice cube may seem like one solid chunk. But it's really made of hydrogen and oxygen atoms. Those atoms connect to form groups called **molecules**. Chemistry is the study of molecules and what happens when different types of molecules get together.

You're about to learn how to put chemistry to work to do some pretty cool things. Move over, boys! The girls are ready to discover that science rocks!

atom: an element in its smallest form
molecule: the atoms making up the smallest unit of a substance; H_2O is a molecule of water

   To have the most fun with these projects, just follow a few simple guidelines:
1. Read the project all the way through before you start.
2. Gather all the materials you need.
3. If you don't get the results you expect the first time, try it again. The experiment might work a different way the next time.
4. Have fun!

Festive Fountain

Showcase some chemistry at your next party with this lively centerpiece. It starts out as a simple, colorful decoration. But when you're ready for the real action, just drop in some baking soda.

Supplies

- funnel
- clear 20-ounce plastic bottle
- liquid measuring cup
- 1 cup (240 mililiter) water
- 1 cup (240 mL) white vinegar
- food coloring, any color
- large clear bowl
- measuring spoons
- 1 tablespoon (15 mL) baking soda

1. Put the funnel into the bottle. Measure the water and vinegar, and pour into the bottle.

2. Remove the funnel. Add four drops of food coloring to the bottle. Swirl the bottle around gently to mix in the color.

3. Stand the bottle inside the clear bowl, and set them out with your party decorations.

4. Once your party is under way, measure the baking soda and pour it into the bottle. Watch the fun overflow!

Insider Info

Adding baking soda to the mixture in the bottle starts a **chemical reaction**. When mixed, baking soda and vinegar make carbon dioxide **gas**. The gas forms bubbles in the water. The bubbles form so quickly that they come pouring out.

chemical reaction: a mixing of chemicals to make something new

gas: something that is not solid or liquid and does not have a definite shape

Bubblicious Fun

Bubble baths are fun and relaxing. They also show off the unusual chemistry of water. Use that chemistry to make a sudsy gift to share.

Supplies

- liquid measuring cup
- ½ cup (120 mL) liquid baby soap
- ½ cup (120 mL) water
- small bowl
- spoon
- measuring spoons
- 1 tablespoon (15 mL) glycerin (available in pharmacies)
- ¼ teaspoon (1.2 mL) unsweetened powdered drink mix, any flavor
- 2 3-ounce (89-mL) shampoo bottles
- funnel
- 2 colored note cards
- hole punch
- marker, any color
- ruler
- scissors
- 2 8-inch (20-centimeter) pieces of thin ribbon

1. Measure the baby soap and water, and pour into a small bowl. Stir gently.

2. Measure the glycerin and powdered drink mix. Pour into the soap mixture and stir.

3. Take the lids off the bottles. Place the funnel into one of the plastic bottles. Fill the bottle with the bubble solution. Repeat with the other bottle. Put the lids on tightly.

4 Fold the note cards in half. Punch a hole in the top corner near the fold of each card.

5 Inside each card write the following instructions. *Directions for use: Turn on the water in your bathtub. Pour bubble bath under the running water.*

6 Measure and cut the pieces of ribbon. Thread them through the holes in the cards. Tie one ribbon around each bottle. Give your bubbly gift to a friend or family member. Or keep a bottle for yourself for some sudsy stress relief.

Insider Info

Water molecules really know how to stick together. You've probably seen them beading up into water droplets on the sides of your tub. Water molecules have such a strong attraction to each other that it's hard to get them to let go. This attraction is called **cohesion**. The molecular cohesion in pure water is too strong to let air inside. But the molecules in baby soap can change that. The soap molecules have one end that attracts water and one that pushes water away. The soap loosens the water's grip just enough to let it hold air. Then the glycerin steps in to keep the water from **evaporating** very quickly. And what's air surrounded by water? A bubble!

cohesion: the act of sticking together tightly
evaporate: to change from a liquid into a vapor or a gas

Peppermint Lip Balm

Here's a sight for sore lips. Smooth this lip balm onto dry, chapped lips. And take advantage of the fact that oil and water don't mix.

Supplies

- measuring spoons
- 1 teaspoon (5 mL) grated or chopped beeswax (available at craft stores)
- 2 teaspoons (10 mL) olive oil
- 1 teaspoon (5 mL) honey
- small microwaveable bowl
- craft stick
- pot holders
- ¼ teaspoon (1.2 mL) peppermint extract
- empty baby food jar or lip balm tin

1. Measure and pour the beeswax, olive oil, and honey into a small microwaveable bowl.

2. Microwave on high for 30 seconds. If the beeswax is not melted, stir it with the craft stick and microwave for 20 more seconds. Use pot holders to hold the hot bowl.

3 Measure and add the peppermint extract to the beeswax mixture. Stir with the craft stick. If you don't like peppermint, try vanilla extract instead.

4 Pour the solution into an empty baby food jar or lip balm tin. Let cool until it is solid.

Insider Info

The fact that oil and water don't mix is helpful when it comes to dry lips. The substances don't mix because their molecules are too different to join together. Water molecules have an uneven electrical **charge**. One side of a water molecule has a small negative charge. The other side has a small positive charge. The negative side of one water molecule sticks to the positive side of another one. Oil molecules don't have positive and negative sides. They don't have a way to stick to the water molecules. So the two substances stay separate. In the lip balm, the wax spreads out the oil molecules and helps them stick to skin. The olive oil forms a barrier on your lips that water can't cross. The water stays in, and your lips don't dry out.

charge: a measure of electricity

Vanilla-Almond Shampoo

Great hair starts with great shampoo. And the secret to shampoo is all in the molecules.

Supplies

- liquid measuring cup
- 1½ cups (360 mL) water
- small saucepan
- pot holder
- measuring spoons
- 1 tablespoon (15 mL) grated Ivory or clear glycerin soap
- spoon
- 2 tablespoons (30 mL) glycerin
- ¼ teaspoon (1.2 mL) almond extract
- ½ teaspoon (2.5 mL) vanilla extract
- funnel
- clean empty shampoo bottle

1. Measure and pour the water into the saucepan. Have an adult boil the water. Remove pan from the heat and set on a pot holder.

2. Measure the soap, and stir it into the hot water until it's **dissolved**.

3. Measure the glycerin and almond and vanilla extracts. Stir all into the soap mixture.

4. Put the funnel in the bottle. Pour in the shampoo. The mixture will thicken as it cools. In 20 minutes, you can hop in the shower and give it a try.

Insider Info

As you learned from the lip balm, oil doesn't dissolve in water. So plain water can't wash oily dirt out of your hair. Soap molecules, however, serve as a bridge between the two. One end of a soap molecule dissolves in water. The other end dissolves in oils. When you put shampoo in your wet hair, the soap molecules connect to both the oil and the water. When you rinse out the soap, the soap molecules drag the oily dirt out as well.

dissolve: to disappear into something else

Stress-Relieving Putty

Take a bottle of glue, and turn it into something new. You'll stretch, bounce, and knead your stress away with this squishy putty.

Supplies

- measuring spoons
- 1 tablespoon (15 mL) borax (available near laundry detergents)
- large bowl
- liquid measuring cup
- 4 cups (960 mL) hot tap water
- spoon
- 1 1.25-fluid ounce (37-mL) bottle of white school glue
- paper towels
- food coloring, any color
- small plastic zip-top bag

1. Measure the borax and pour into a large bowl.

2. Measure and pour the hot water into the bowl with the borax. Stir together.

3. Squeeze all the glue into the bowl in a spiral motion.

14

4. When all of the glue is floating in the bowl, scoop it out with your hands. Squish it into a ball.

5. Press the ball between paper towels to remove the extra water.

6. Stretch the putty out flat, and put one drop of food coloring in the middle. Fold the putty over to cover up the coloring. Then knead the putty until the color is mixed in evenly.

7. Try stretching, squishing, and bouncing your new ball of putty. Store it in a sealed plastic bag when you are done.

Insider Info

Glue molecules are **polymers**. Polymers are long molecules with repeating groups of atoms. Think of them as a chain of paper clips linked end to end. Now imagine you have two paper clip chains. Link those two chains together by attaching an extra paper clip to the middle of each chain. This linking of chains is what borax does to the glue. As you knead the glue ball, the chains then get all tangled up. They turn into a solid putty instead of staying liquid glue.

polymer: tiny pieces of matter that have repeating groups of atoms linked together

Earth-Friendly Plastic

You can use milk to make an all-natural plastic necklace. Unlike regular plastics, this one won't stay in the environment forever.

Supplies

- liquid measuring cup
- 1 cup (240 mL) milk
- measuring spoons
- 1 tablespoon (15 mL) white vinegar
- small microwaveable bowl
- spoon
- strainer
- paper towels
- wax paper
- small cookie cutter, any shape
- pencil
- paint, glitter, or other decorations
- ruler
- scissors
- 20-inch (51-cm) piece of thin ribbon

1. Measure and pour the milk and vinegar into a small microwavable bowl.

2. Microwave on high for one minute. Stir. You should see lumps appearing in the milk. If no lumps form, microwave for another 30 seconds.

3. Pour the milk through a strainer to catch the lumps. When they're cool enough to touch, scrape the lumps into a ball with your hands. Squeeze the ball between two paper towels to get rid of any extra liquid.

4. On a piece of wax paper, press the milk solids into a cookie cutter. Carefully lift the cutter, and push out the shape.

5. Make a hole near the top of the shape with a pencil.

6. Allow the shape to dry completely. Drying will take about three days.

7. If you like, paint and decorate the shape. Let dry.

8. Measure and cut the ribbon. Thread it through the hole in the shape. Tie the ribbon around your neck.

Insider Info

Remember the Little Miss Muffet nursery rhyme? She ate curds and whey. Well, that lumpy stuff you made in the microwave is curds and whey. Heat and vinegar made the milk separate into two parts. The liquid part is the whey, and the solid parts are curds. Curds contain a polymer that is similar to plastic. Plastic polymers are usually made from crude oil. But very few **microorganisms** can digest oil. Milk is in the diets of a lot more microorganisms. So with enough time and moisture, microorganisms will break down milk plastic. When your style changes, toss the milk plastic pendant into the compost bin instead of the garbage. However, if you decorate the milk plastic with paint or glitter don't put it in the compost bin. The paint or decorations won't break down like the milk plastic and shouldn't be composted.

microorganism: a living thing too small to be seen without a microscope

Apple-Cinnamon Air Freshener

A sweet scent is the perfect finish for a clean room. Raid your kitchen for some fragrant ingredients. Then use this air freshener to spread cinnamon molecules far and wide.

Supplies

- measuring spoons
- rubber spatula
- 4 tablespoons (60 mL) applesauce
- 4 tablespoons (60 mL) cinnamon
- small bowl
- wax paper
- cookie cutter, any shape
- pencil
- ruler
- scissors
- 8-inch (20-cm) piece of string

1. Measure and mix the applesauce and cinnamon in a small bowl. Stir until it forms a thick paste.

2. Dump the mixture onto wax paper.

3. Spread the batter out until it is about ½ inch (13 millimeters) thick.

4. Use the cookie cutter to cut a shape into the batter.

5. Peel the extra batter away from the cookie cutter. Poke a hole at the top of the shape with the pencil. Then remove the cookie cutter.

6. Let it dry for several days until it is hard.

7. Measure and cut the string. Thread it through the hole, and knot the ends. Hang it up for some good-smelling décor.

Insider Info

You won't have to stick your nose right on your air freshener to get a sweet smell. Molecules naturally spread out from where there are many to where there are fewer. This action is called **diffusion**. Your air freshener has a lot of cinnamon molecules. Over time, they spread out to fill the room. When those molecules hit your nose, you smell cinnamon.

diffusion: mixing together of different substances caused by the random motion of molecules and atoms

Rainbow Candle Holders

Pick up some red cabbage for your next party centerpiece. Yes, cabbage! With a little chemistry know-how, you can turn cabbage juice from drab to fab.

Supplies

- 6 leaves of red cabbage
- large microwaveable bowl
- liquid measuring cup
- 4 cups (960 mL) distilled water
- pot holders
- spoon
- slotted spoon
- 4 clear glasses
- measuring spoons
- 4 tablespoons (60 mL) white vinegar
- 2 teaspoons (10 mL) baking soda
- 2 tablespoons (30 mL) window cleaner
- 4 floating candles

1. Tear the cabbage leaves into small pieces. Put them in a large microwaveable bowl.

2. Measure the water, and pour it over the leaves. Microwave on high for five minutes. Use pot holders to take the bowl out of the microwave. Then stir the water and leaves. Let the cabbage soak in the hot water for one hour.

3. Using a slotted spoon, remove the cabbage leaves and throw away. Pour ⅔ cup (160 mL) cabbage juice into each of the four glasses.

4 Measure the vinegar. Pour it into one of the glasses. Stir the mixture with a spoon, and watch the magic!

5 Measure the baking soda. Pour it into another glass and stir.

6 Measure the window cleaner, and add it to a third glass and stir.

7 Keep one glass of pure cabbage juice.

8 Line up the glasses, and add a floating candle to each one. Let the colors of chemistry shine!

Insider Info

Red cabbage contains a colored molecule called a pigment. The shape of the pigment molecule determines what color it will be. When the pigment is in a neutral solution, such as water, it looks purple. But in an **acid** like vinegar, a chemical reaction changes the shape of the molecule. It looks pink. When mixed with a **base** like baking soda, the pigment changes to a different shape. This one appears blue. A very strong base, like the ammonia in window cleaner, makes the same molecule look green. Red cabbage juice is a chemical that can be used to show if something is an acid or a base.

acid: a chemical that tastes sour and reacts easily with bases
base: a chemical that tastes bitter and reacts easily with acids

The Great Muffin Puff

Compare two batches of dough in this muffin bake-off. The first has a little baking powder. The second has lots more. Which one will rise to the occasion?

Supplies

- paper muffin liners
- muffin tin with space for 12 muffins
- measuring spoons
- ⅓ cup plus 4 tablespoons (140 mL) sugar, divided
- small bowl
- 1½ teaspoons (7.5 mL) cinnamon
- spoon
- large bowl
- dry-ingredient measuring cups
- 2 cups (480 mL) flour
- 1 teaspoon (5 mL) salt
- 3 tablespoons (45 mL) baking powder, divided
- liquid measuring cup
- 1 cup (240 mL) milk
- ⅓ cup (80 mL) vegetable oil
- 1 egg
- ¼ cup (60 mL) water

1. Put 12 paper liners in a muffin tin. Have an adult preheat the oven to 350 degrees Fahrenheit (176 degrees Celsius.)

2. Measure and pour 4 tablespoons (60 mL) sugar into a small bowl. Measure and add the cinnamon to the bowl. Stir ingredients together, then set bowl aside.

3. In a large bowl, measure and mix the flour, salt, remaining sugar, and 1 tablespoon (15 mL) of baking powder.

4. Measure the milk and oil and add to the flour mixture. Add the egg, and mix altogether.

continue on next page

5. Put ⅓ cup (80 mL) of this batter into each of six muffin liners.

6. Measure and add 2 tablespoons (30 mL) baking powder and the water to the leftover batter. Stir.

7. Fill each of the remaining muffin liners with ⅓ cup (80 mL) of the batter.

8. Sprinkle a bit of the cinnamon and sugar mixture on top of each muffin.

9. With an adult's help, bake the muffins for 12-15 minutes or until a fork inserted in the middle comes out clean. Watch the muffins through the oven window to see how they rise!

10. When they're done, dig in. Both types will be edible, but the muffins with the extra baking powder may not be very tasty.

Insider Info

In the Festive Fountain experiment, we saw how the base baking soda and the acid vinegar react together. When combined they create carbon dioxide gas. Baking powder is a combination of baking soda and other ingredients that form an acid when they get wet. As you mix the batter, tiny carbon dioxide bubbles form, and the dough begins to rise. When muffins have too much baking powder, extra carbon dioxide is formed. The bread puffs up high at first. But then the muffin tops collapse under their own weight.

Sweet Jewels

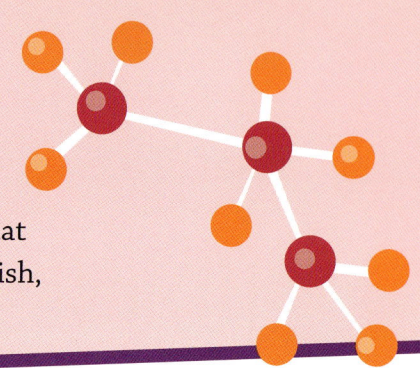

What's better than a treat you can wear and eat? Making that treat yourself, of course! This project will take a few days to finish, but it will be well worth the wait.

Supplies

- dry-ingredient measuring cups
- 2¾ cups (660 mL) sugar
- small saucepan
- liquid measuring cup
- 1 cup (240 mL) water
- spoon
- food coloring, any color
- scissors
- string
- tall clean jar, such as a quart jar
- pencil
- paper clip
- funnel
- plastic wrap
- ruler

1. Measure and add the sugar to the small saucepan. Measure and pour the water into the pan.

2. Have an adult heat the water and sugar on medium-high heat. Stir continuously to keep the sugar from burning. As the water begins to boil, the sugar will dissolve, and the solution will look clear.

3 Once the sugar has dissolved, add 10 drops of food coloring and stir. Remove the pot from the heat, and let it cool for 10 minutes.

4 While the pot cools, cut a piece of string about as long as your jar is tall. Tie the string around the middle of a pencil.

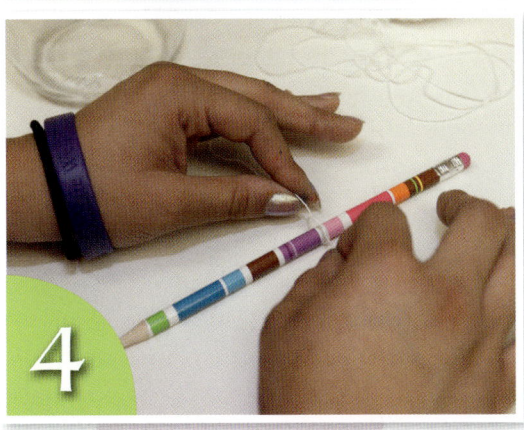

5 Lay the pencil across the top of the jar so the string hangs into the jar. Trim the string if it touches the bottom of the jar.

6 Take the string out of the jar. Slide the paper clip onto the bottom of the string as if you were sliding it onto a stack of papers. Set the pencil and string aside for later.

continue on next page

7 When the sugar solution has cooled, skim any solid sugar off the top and throw away. Then using the funnel, pour the sugar solution into your jar.

8 Lay the pencil back across the jar so that the string and paper clip sink into the sugar solution.

9 Loosely cover the jar with plastic wrap over the pencil. Then set the jar aside. Crystals will start to grow along the string within 24 hours. In seven days, you should have a thick pendant of rock candy.

10 Rinse the pendant briefly under cool water, and pat it dry. Measure and cut a piece of string about 20 inches (51 cm) long. Tie it to the top of the pendant, and hang it around your neck. You have a candy necklace!

Insider Info

Look closely at your rock candy. You'll see rectangles and squares with smooth, flat sides. These shapes are crystals. Crystals form when you dissolve lots of sugar in just a little water. You heated the water because more sugar can dissolve in hot water than in cold. Heat gives sugar extra energy for dissolving. But as the water cools, the sugar loses that energy. Some of the sugar turns back into a solid. The rough string provides a good surface for sugar molecules to hang onto as they solidify. Sugar molecules all have the same shape. They connect neatly to each other like a stack of building blocks. The whole process happens slowly enough that the sugar molecules build up into large, beautiful crystals.

Glossary

acid (A-suhd)—a chemical that tastes sour and reacts easily with bases

atom (AT-uhm)—an element in its smallest form

base (BAYS)—a chemical that tastes bitter and reacts easily with acids

charge (CHARJ)—a measure of electricity

chemical reaction (KE-muh-kuhl ree-AK-shuhn)—a mixing of chemicals to make something new

cohesion (ko-HE-zhun)—the act of sticking together tightly

diffusion (dih-FYOO-zhuhn)—mixing together of different substances caused by the random motion of molecules and atoms

dissolve (di-ZOLV)—to disappear into something else

evaporate (i-VA-puh-rayt)—to change from a liquid into a vapor or a gas

gas (GASS)—something that is not solid or liquid and does not have a definite shape

microorganism (mye-kro-OR-gan-iz-um)—a living thing too small to be seen without a microscope

molecule (MOL-uh-kyool)—the atoms making up the smallest unit of a substance; H_2O is a molecule of water

polymer (POL-uh-mur)—tiny pieces of matter that have repeating groups of atoms linked together; there are natural polymers and human-made polymers

Read More

Eagen, Rachel. *Body Care Chemistry*. Chemtastophe! New York.: Crabtree Pub., 2011.

O'Neal, Claire. *A Project Guide to Chemistry*. Physical Science Projects for Kids. Hockessin, Del.: Mitchell Lane Publishers, 2011.

Walker, Pamela and Elaine Wood. *Chemistry Experiments*. Science Experiments. New York: Facts on File, 2011.

Internet Sites

FactHound offers a safe, fun way to find Internet sites related to this book. All of the sites on FactHound have been researched by our staff.

Here's all you do:

Visit www.facthound.com

Type in this code: 9781429676748

 Check out projects, games and lots more at www.capstonekids.com

Index

acids, 21, 25
atoms, 4, 15
attraction, 9, 11

bases, 21, 25
bubbles, 7, 8–9, 25

carbon dioxide, 7, 25
charges, 11
chemical reactions, 7, 21
cohesion, 9
crystals, 28, 29

diffusion, 18–19

evaporation, 9

molecules, 4, 9, 11, 12–13, 15, 18–19, 21, 29

oils, 10–11, 13

pigments, 21
plastics, 16–17
polymers, 15, 17

water, 8–9, 10–11, 13, 21

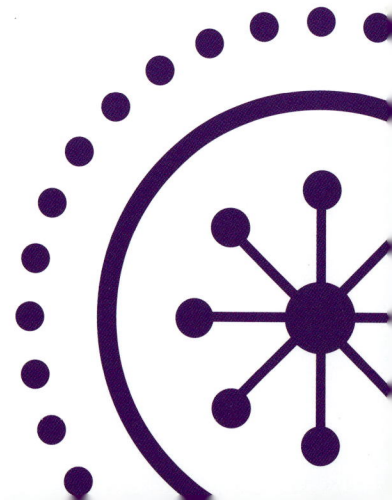